A Guide To Sensual F*cking

Learn To Give Your Woman, Hard And Sensual, Just The Way She Wants!

ROMAN ALYSSA

Limit of Liability

The information in this book is solely for informational purposes, not as a medical instruction to replace the advice of your physician or as a replacement for any treatment prescribed by your physician. The author and publisher do not take responsibility for any possible consequences from any treatment, procedure, exercise, dietary modification, action or application of medication which results from reading or following the information contained in this book.

If you are ill or suspect that you have a medical problem, we strongly encourage you to consult your medical, health, or other competent professional before adopting any of the suggestions in this book or drawing inferences from it.

This book and the author's opinions are solely for informational and educational purposes. The author specifically disclaims all responsibility for any liability, loss, or risk, personal or otherwise which is incurred as a consequence, directly or indirectly, of the use and application of any of the contents of this book.

ISBN-13: 978-1523948406

ISBN-10: 152394840X

DEDICATION

To all who desire to enjoy the very best from a fulfilling
sex life with their lovers, and live life to the fullest!

TABLE OF CONTENT

INTRODUCTION

As a relationship activist and sex coach, author, mother and wife. Years ago I was bored with my sex life; I was exhausted, unhappy and desperately aching for a better relationship with my spouse sexually. One day, gruelingly tired of my situation, I started researching everything I could on sex and creative sex positions and transforming me and my husband's sex life. I soon found out and decided to share with you in very clear straight to the point terms.

I'm tempted to say buying this book might just be about the best thing you have done lately, now don't mind me; I know you have bought other good stuffs. This is one book that is founded by a great passion to see lovers enjoy creative sex and explore new sex positions.

Many couples just oscillate between two or less sex positions and it's becoming something of a great worry. As they are getting tired of regular stuffs, and are fast becoming bored with how limited those few sex positions can be.

This book is just right for you; you made a great choice getting a copy. Enjoy reading through its pages as much as I had fun writing it and have fun with your lover.

Basset Hound Sex Position

This position is a variation of the Doggy Style. It is named so because of the closeness of the couples to the floor. The position is straightforward; the woman is on all fours with the man holding on to the woman's bottom or the sides. Because of the low position the woman's rear is pushed right back, while the man's knees is placed to either side of the buttocks. The low position requires a degree of flexibility in the couple's hips and may not be comfortable for many couples but for those who can, the effort is really fun!

Ben Dover Sex Position

The woman needs to lean forward & balance with her hands, while the man holds his woman from behind. The woman needs a little flexibility and a bit of leg strength to perform this position well.

Both couple needs to face in the same direction while standing upright. The man then needs to enter the woman. When he has penetrated her, he then needs to lean over and stretch her arms out until she is touching the floor with them to balance herself. Ideally, she should try to keep her hands as close to her feet as possible, but if the woman is not that flexible or it feels uncomfortable, then you are free to lean forward a bit.

The Leapfrog Position

This position is also known as Froggy style. It is an interesting variation of doggy style sex position. In this position, the woman squats down but rather than getting into regular Doggy style sex position on all fours, the woman lowers her forearms to the ground and raises her butt so she can be penetrated entered by her man from behind. This position can be used for vaginal or anal sex. The man should support his woman's waist to help her weight. This position could take an extent of flexibility to perform.

Corner Cowgirl Sex Position

This sex position is a variation of the popular Cowgirl sex position, where the woman is on top of her man at the corner of the bed, while her man lies on his back. This is a position is fun to try out with your spouse.

The man has to lie on his back on the bed. His crotch is positioned by the corner of the bed, so that one of his legs dangles over one side of the bed, while the other leg dangles over the end of the bed. The man should plant his feet on the floor to give him some stability. The woman then needs to straddle him as she normally would when performing the cowgirl position so that she is on her knees, "bouncing" up and down on him.

Crab Sex Position

This sex position is a position that I will only recommend to couples in which the man has a good penile flexibility. The reason is because the woman will be bending his penis really far back when she sits on him.

The Crab Sex Position is in many ways very similar to the Cowgirl position, with the woman on her knees on top, facing her man while he lies on his back. Instead of the woman being in a semi upright position on top of her man, she will be leaning right back. She should make sure that she stretches her hands out behind her to support herself in this position. Her man should keep his legs together.

Fast Fuck Sex Position

As the name suggests this sex position is perfect when you want a quickie with your man. The Fast Fuck involves the man rapidly thrusting in and out. In many ways, the Fast Fuck is somehow similar to the woman on top position or even the Asian Cowgirl position.

The man lies down on his back and then he bends his knees slightly with his feet planted on the ground. The woman then straddles him. She has a choice of being on her knees or on her feet; the decision is up to her. But she will be leaning forward, resting on her hands or elbows. She needs to position herself so that she is slightly raised above her man.

Jugghead Sex Position

This position is likely the craziest looking sex making positions that you may see, even though to perform it is not as difficult.

The couple is going to need to use either a couch or a bed to do the jugghead position. The man would need to set himself up first. The man lies down beside the bed/couch with his back on the floor.

The man then puts his legs up on the sofa or the bed. The woman then needs to position herself above him on all fours with one arm and one leg on the either side of him. The man now needs to lift his crotch and lower his back off the floor and then start penetrating the woman, while she thrusts back onto him.

Lunge Sex Position

This position's name originated from the way it is performed. The woman will be lunging on top of her man while performing it. This means that she needs to have some flexibility and strength if she wants to perform the Lunge for an extensive time with her man. Some folks see the Lunge as a novel sex position while some other folks see it as a regular sex position.

The man has to lie down on his back on the bed and he needs to open his legs. The women would then get into a lunging position on top of the man. She sets out to achieve this by standing up straight on the bed, facing the man with her feet together just below his crotch with her feet inside his legs.

Then she takes her left foot and then places it to the side of her man's right arm on the bed. Next she puts her right leg backwards behind herself so that she is in a lunging position and she lowers herself onto her man. With help from her man, she slowly lowers and raises herself on her man while he is inside her.

Missionary

This position is also known as the Male Dominant or the Matrimonial.

This is also the most used position in the world. It is an intimate position that allows face to face contact. The woman lies on the bed and the man lays on top of her, the woman could spread her legs wide open or she raise her knees and digs her feet in the mattress. The man likes it because he can control the depth of penetration and the speed of thrusting. She enjoys feeling the man's weight on her body, and the skin to skin contact. The only little downside of this position is that this position can make it more difficult to hold off ejaculation because of the intense friction and deep thrusting.

Rodeo sex

This sex position is a sex game of sorts, a sex game that you can only play once with a partner

Rodeo sex involves entering a girl from the back doggy style and reaching around and taking hold of her breasts. Once you are well inside of her, lean forward and whisper into her ear "I love you, Nichola" Or any other name that ISN'T her's, or you could say "that's how your sister loves it too" or "that's how Sarah moans too"

The fun of the game now comes from seeing how long the man can hold on in her while she kicks trying to get you off.

Sybian Sex Position

This position got its name from the Sybian machine. It is a vibrator in a box that the woman straddles in a manner resembling the Cowgirl position, with a knee on either of the sides of it on the bed.

The Sybian sex position is similar to this idea above, but it has few differences. The first is that the man will be on either a bed of cushions or a soft cushioned stool or the seat. He will be lying on his butt.

This position can get very tiring, very quickly for the man. The woman will need something that her man can comfortably lie on that doesn't have any armrests that would inconvenient him.

The woman will still be straddling her man like in the Cowgirl position, except instead of resting on her knees on either side of her man, she will be on her feet, sitting in his lap while facing him. She can put her hands on her man or on either side of him to help keep herself balanced.

Thigh Tide Sex Position

This position is really fun and very easy to perform it. It's a great position to try out.

The man needs to lie on his back with his legs straight and also spread slightly apart. Now he raises one of knee slightly and then plants his foot on the bed. The woman now then puts one knee on either side of his bent leg and then he sit down on his crotch while facing away from him. The woman now uses her legs to raise herself up and down on the man. She makes sure to hold onto her man's leg to help steady herself. It is really great for slow and sensual sex!

Delight Sex Position

This sex position is a great for couples who want to be quite intimate. The position is also very nice because you don't have to put in that much effort to perform the Delight.

The woman needs to sit at either the edge of her bed or on a sofa or on the edge of any surface that is about twelve to twenty inches from the ground. When she is sitting down, she opens her legs wide. Her man then kneels in front of her, facing her. For the man to enter her, she may need to slightly lower herself over the edge. Her man will usually have his legs close together. He can then grab her waist or legs as he is thrusting into her.

High Chair Sex Position

This position is a fun position, a rear entry sex position, where the woman gets to sit and relax literally, while her man is the one who does most of the work. The only thing she will need to perform the position with her man is a tall stool or a bar stool

The woman is going to be sitting down on a tall stool or bar stool with her butt hanging out over the edge. So she is going to be sitting on the underside of her thighs, not her butt. The man will enter her from behind. Then she can now lean forwards away from her man or backwards into her man to find the right angle. If her man is not tall enough to penetrate her, then get your man to stand on something firm.

Don't put anything under the bar stool you are using, making sure it is on a firm, solid surface to prevent any accidents.

Ballerina Sex Position

This position is one of those super exotic ones that ninety five percent of women or ladies will just never be able to perform. This is simply because flexibility is key in this position. However if you get to performing it, then it can be very intimate and pleasurable.

The couple needs to start by facing each other while standing. The woman is now going to need to raise one of her legs upwards until she is resting it on her man's shoulder, while balancing on her other leg. Her leg that is resting on the man's shoulder is going to be almost straight, allowing the woman to be very close to her man.

Sofa Surprise Sex Position

This sex position sounds like the name. It can only be performed on a sofa, but it can also be performed when on an armchair, in bed or even on the floor. In many different ways it's very similar to the Asian Cowgirl

The man sits on a sofa as he would normally. The woman then squats down from a standing position on the sofa while she faces towards him so that he can penetrate her. She will be squatting quite far down, so she needs a little bit of flexibility otherwise it will be uncomfortable. If you are doing the Sofa Surprise on a bed, then the man will have to sit against the headboard and should put in a few pillows behind him for support.

Burning Man Sex Position

This position got the name from the fact that it is a passionate, fiery, 'burning' sex between the couples in this position. To do it, you will need either a counter top or table.

The woman needs to face the counter top and then lay her stomach over it while keeping her feet on the ground. The man can then penetrate her from behind either vaginally or anally. As her legs remain on the ground, they will act as an anchor, keeping her in place so that the man can really give her some hard, intense penetration without her slipping out of place.

Lap Dance

Get a tall-backed chair, pad the chair with some pillows, and sit the man down. Then straddle his hardened member and leaning back slightly, the woman placing her hands on the man's knees. Extending her legs, one at a time, until each of her ankles is resting on one of his corresponding shoulders. The woman pumps her booty back and forth at a speed that makes her moan. To super charge her thrusting power, balancing her weight between her ankles and her hands.

Pump Sex Position

In this position, the woman straddles a chair, with the man crouches on the chair seat behind her. The woman would stabilize the chair by holding its back, because care should be taken not to tip the chair and the man over in the excitement.

It is important to use a very good chair.

Slow Dance Sex Position

This sex position is a really fun position for the man and woman, where the couple is standing up. Well thankfully it's not as difficult as some other positions.

The couple needs to be standing while facing each other. If the man is taller than the woman, then the man needs to bend his knees and get a little lower than her so that he can enter her. To help the man to enter her, she will need to open her legs a bit. Then both of you just need to wrap your arms around each other and the man can thrust up into his woman. This position is great for slow intimate sex, while standing up.

If the woman is far smaller than the man, the Slow Dance will be impossible to perform unless she is standing on a stairs. But if she is taller than the man, then she can bend her knees and lower herself on the man.

Washing Machine Sex Position

This sex position actually needs a piece of equipment and that's a washing machine.

Find a washing machine, put few dirty clothes inside it and turn it on to a high spin setting. Then the woman needs to lean over the washing machine while still standing just like in the Burning Man Sex position. This will help to bring the woman's groin area in closer contact with the vibrating washing machine. The man will then enter her from m behind and start thrusting into her while standing.

Betty Rocker Sex Position

This position is one that most couples may never ever even come to trying. It may look a little out of this world, but it actually comes easy to perform.

The man needs to lie flat on the bed with his legs spread just a little bit apart. The woman then needs to straddle the man, but instead of facing him, she turns around, so that your man is now looking at your back. While upright, the woman slides his penis inside her, so that she is now in the Asian Cowgirl position with him. Once he is inside her, she starts to lean forwards slowly and rest part of her weight on her arms or his legs.

It is important to remember to start slowly in the Betty Rocker position so that she doesn't accidentally hurt her man!

Now the woman then starts rocking forwards and backwards on her arms and legs. But the fun doesn't stop there, the woman can also move herself up and down on her man's penis or he can thrust into her if rocking doesn't do it for her.

Bridge Sex Position

This position is a little stressful and you may be unable to last more than two minutes. It can be categorized among sexercise.

The woman needs to get into the 'crab' position that is used in gymnastics. The woman would be on all fours, except that her back will be facing the ground or the bed. The man now needs to get onto his knees between her legs while facing her. He then enters her and puts his hand on her thighs to help pull her towards him with each thrust. Keeping herself elevated in this position is very tiring.

Chair Riding Sex Position

This position is somehow exotic and takes two chairs to do it. If you do not use the right chairs for this position, you may find it to be quite uncomfortable.

This sex position takes fairly longer to set up than most other positions. First get two chairs so that they are facing each other, they should be near each other, so that they are almost touching each other. The man now needs to sit down on one and open his legs quite wide. The woman now needs to sit down on the other with her legs close together. The couple will both be facing each other for this position. Now the woman needs to slowly bring herself towards his penis while he brings his penis closer to her vagina. The woman will find that lifting her legs upwards will make it a whole lot easier. She may even find that putting her ankles over his shoulders like she would when performing the Octopus position makes it a lot more comfortable for her. Her man then holds onto her legs or grab her arms to gently thrust into her.

G-Spot Sniper Sex Position

The G-Spot Sniper position might look really unconventional but if you stick to it, you are and your man would really enjoy a great deal of experience.

The woman tries locking her feet together behind her man's neck to help her lift her lower body off the bed. The man then helps to keep her raised using his hands under her waist.

The woman needs to start off having sex with her man like she would in the Deep Impact sex position. This means that she needs to lie on her back while on the bed with her legs in the air, pointing at the ceiling. The man will be penetrating her while on his knees. But instead of spreading his knees apart to lower himself down towards his woman like in many other sex positions, the man needs to keep his knees together so that he is as tall as possible.

The man will then grab his woman by her legs or knees and pull her up towards him so that he can penetrate her. Almost all of the entire body will now be pointing towards the ceiling and the woman will carry all of her weight on her shoulders or upper back while holding onto her man's legs to steady herself.

The G Spot Sniper position is a little tasking, and it's not advisable to do this position if you have a bad back.

Jellyfish Sex Position

The Jellyfish is a little more difficult adaptation of the Kneeling Missionary. In this position, the man kneels up slightly while the woman sits into their lap, also facing him. The woman wraps their legs around the man; the couple wraps their arms around each other for support. This provides a better angle for penetration.

The couple together sets up a fluid rocking motion to gain movement during penetration - this resulting visually in a jelly fish kind of fluid movement, hence the name Jellyfish.

Life Raft Sex Position

This position may sound like a novel sex position for couples at first. But it's very pleasurable for several reasons.

The woman needs one of those inflatable pool mattresses that you can lie on. Some people call it 'lilos', some others call them inflatable pool beds. The woman needs to lie on her stomach on the mattress and in a pool, with her vagina in the middle of the mattress, while she is in the shallow water. The man then straddles her, with his feet on the bottom of the pool so that he is not sitting on the woman, pushing the woman downwards, but rather he is standing over the woman. He then enters her and starts to thrust.

Coital alignment technique (CAT)

This sex position a.k.a "grinding the corn", this sex position is primarily used as a variation of the regular missionary position and it is also structured to increase the chances of stimulating the clitoris during sexual intercourse (coitus). This can be achieved by combining the "riding high" variation of the missionary position with pressure-counterpressure movements performed by the couple in rhythm with coitus.

When this sex position is used as a variant of the missionary position, the man has to lie above the woman but he also moves upward along the body of the woman, until his erection begins to point down, and the dorsal side of the man's penis starts to press against the clitoris; and unlike in the regular missionary position, the man's body moves downward (relative to the woman's) during the inward stroke, and upward for the outward stroke. The woman may also wrap her legs around the man's. Sexual movement is focused around the pelvises, without leverage from the arms or legs. The rocking upward stroke (where the woman leads) and downward stroke (where the man leads) of sexual movement builds arousal that couple let develop and peak naturally.

Note the woman on top variant is known as the reverse coital alignment technique.

Little Dipper Sex Position

This position is a novel position that is more like a Sexercise than some great sex. This sex position is the sister version of the Big Dipper Sex position. This position requires strength to perform. But to save energy, the woman should rest down on her man's lap and let him do the thrusting.

The woman needs a sofa or a bed and a footstool or sturdy chair. The man lies down on the floor on his back in between the bed and footstool. The woman now positions herself over the man and sits down on his crotch. The woman need now places her feet on the footstool and her hands behind her on the bed. The woman is now going to lift herself up and down on her man using her arms like she would if she were in the gym and she was performing bench dips.

Octopus Sex Position

This position is one you may have never heard anything of. That's cool because it's a new thing to try between couples.

The man sits down on the floor and lean backwards slightly; the man uses his hands placed behind his back to support himself. He will find balance if his legs is spread. The man now bends his legs slightly. The woman now stands over him (each foot either side of his waist) and the woman now slowly lowers herself in a squatting position onto his penis. Once he is inside her, she sits on his lap and slowly starts to lean backwards. Placing her hands behind her back on the ground for support. Once she is leaning backwards, she then need to lift her right leg and rest it on her man's left shoulder. Now she lifts her left leg and rests it on his right shoulder.

Pearly Gates Sex Position

This is not one crazy position that requires lots of gym expertise or strength, though many couples are yet to try it.

The couple will both be facing in the same direction. The man lies on his back on the bed with his knees bent and his feet planted on the bed. The woman lies on top of her man, also on her back with her head above his and to the side while her man penetrates her. So the woman would look like she is Spooning while facing the ceiling. Staying balanced on the man is important, so the woman needs to spread out her legs and bend them so that she can keep her feet on the bed.

The woman should also spread out her arms too to stay balanced. The man can then wrap his arms around her waist or chest or under her arms, grabbing her shoulders.

Piledriver Sex Position

This position is quite an exotic position that requires a lot of time at the gym working on your flexibility. It can somehow awkward to do this position between couples, and once you are in it, it can be really uncomfortable for the couple. Both vaginal and anal sex is possible in this position.

The woman needs to lie on her back. Next she needs to lift her legs in the air. The man now needs to grab the back of her ankles and slowly push them towards her head. This will cause her lower back to start lifting up off the bed. Alternatively if it's comfortable, the man will keep pushing her ankles towards her head until all of her back is off the ground and the only thing that's left on the ground is her shoulders and the back of her head.

This will leave her very exposed (this can be a turn on for some couples). The man now needs to keep at least one of his hands on the woman's ankles so that he can hold her in place. To enter the woman, the man points his penis downwards which can be uncomfortable.

Piston Sex Position

This sex position will fire the couple up without tiring you out (not as compared to the other sexercise oriented positions) Reminiscent of Standing and Carrying, this position has the plus advantages of being very easy on the man's back who happens to be the lifter and more supportive for the woman who would be dangling in the air.

It's worthy of note to know that this position is quite challenging, requiring the standing partner which is the man to be fit and the woman, flexed and focused.

Other conventional sex positions that transits to this position are: Mastery (Suspended and Dancer). Despite our preference; for the man, the man should use proper lifting technique by always bending at the knees, properly keeping his back straight and coming out of the pose very carefully as he went into it ... for the woman, she should hold on as tight as possible and aim to maintain her balance close to her partner.

Sexy scissors sex position

The woman lies face up on a table top or desk with her hips perched on the very edge. She raises her legs to a ninety degree angle, and then the man grabs her ankles. He extends his arms out to his sides, and as the woman's legs are spread-eagle, he enters her while standing. And then, he starts alternately crossing and spreading the woman's legs like scissors, opening and closing as he thrusts into her.

Leg Glider Sex Position

The leg glider is one sex position that needs a lot of gym expertise from the woman, her flexibility should be a great deal, and her man doesn't need to be that flexible to do it.

The woman lies on one side, probably her left side. Meaning that her left leg, left side and left arm will be on the bed. Her right leg will be resting on top of her left leg and her right arm will be resting on her body, although she can put her right hand on the bed to steady herself if she wants. She needs to raise her right leg towards the ceiling while keeping her left leg on the bed. If she is flexible enough, her right leg should be pointing straight towards the ceiling.

Ideally the woman's right legs pointing to the ceiling should be at ninety degrees to the left leg pointing to the wall.

Mongolian Smurf Sex Position

This position is one very enjoyable position with the man on top, where the woman can relax and let her man do pretty much all of the work.

The woman needs to lie on her side in the recovery position just like she would for the Irish Spooning position. Then she raises her top leg a little bit towards her chest and puts her top arm either in front or behind her to stay in position. The woman can keep her lower leg fairly straight and feel free to position her lower arm how she like it. The man now straddles her straight leg while on his knees and remains upright and starts thrusting into the woman. The woman won't be able to do anything in this position so she can just relax and take it easy.

Poles Apart Sex Position

This position provides a lots of G-Spot stimulation without very deep penetration.

The couple lies on their sides, facing in the same direction. This looks like the Spoons position, but it's not. Instead of the woman lying with her head in front of her man's head, she needs to change her position so that her head is now in front of his feet and her feet are in front of his head. In simpler terms the woman should be laying head to toe with her man. The man then enters her from behind either anally or vaginally.

Screw Sex Position

This position is really easy to perform; it's a great one to try out between couples.

The woman starts off by lying on her side to perform the Screw position. Then once she is, she pulls her knees right up to her chest so her groin area is really exposed. The man will then be on his knees facing towards her and will start thrusting her. To get down to the woman's level, the man will need to spread his knees pretty far apart. If he can't, then the woman should try putting a pillow under her hip to raise herself up or the man can can kneel on the floor instead of the bed to get the angles right.

Side Entry Missionary Sex Position

Although it's called the Side Entry Missionary position, it's really doesn't look like the missionary position at all.

The woman lays on her side on the bed with her legs together and bent. Most women are flexible enough in this position to turn and face their man to increase the level of intimacy. Meanwhile the man will be on his knees and will enter the woman from behind. So the man will be in the same position he usually is when performing the missionary position, while the woman will be in a new position.

Sofa Spooning Sex Position

This position is a slight variation of the regular Spooning position. Performing it, a full length and comfortable sofa is needed. Sofa Spooning is good when you are on holidays and want to see movies on TV as you have sex.

The man lies down on the sofa with his back firmly against the backrest part of the sofa. Now the woman lies down in front of him while facing in the same direction. The man now enters her from behind and starts to slowly thrust into her while wrapping his arms around her.

Spoons sex position

This position is also known as spoons position or spooning is a sexual position that derived its name from the way that two spoons may be positioned side by side, with bowls aligned.

In the spoons position one partner lies on one side with knees bent while the other partner lies with his or her front pressed against their back. The spoons cuddling position isn't limited to twosomes.

In this position the woman would be in the inner spoon position and the man is in the outer spoon, preparing to penetrate from the rare. While thrusting, the couples can separate their upper bodies, with just their pelvises connecting; their legs can also rest on top of each other. The woman lifts her upper knee to allow for easier penetration. The man can also caress the woman's stomach and stimulate her breasts, the back of the neck and ears, and clitoris. The woman can also stimulate her own clitoris or the man's scrotum. In addition, the penis stimulates the front of the vagina, and may stimulate an area that is commonly termed the G-spot.

Spork Sex Position

This position is also known as the Spoon and fork Combo. The woman lies on her back, raising her right leg so the man can position himself between her legs at a ninety degree angle and enter her. The woman's legs will form the tines of a Spork, a Spoon-and-fork utensil. The woman can do this with him facing her or facing her back. If the woman is more flexible, she should lift her left leg up to increase the depth of penetration.

From the Spork position, she can lift her top leg and support it by resting it on his shoulder. From this point, she can easily stimulate her clitoris using her fingers while he is inside her.

Woman on top

The woman on top sex position is also known as the riding position or the cowgirl, it is a sex position in which the man sits or lies on his back, and his woman straddles her man with her facing either forward or backward, and her man penetrates the woman in the anus or the vagina.

Twister Sex Position

This position is a very exotic sex position, when you do it; it looks really out of this world. Well for the records just because a lovemaking position may be exotic, doesn't always mean that it is better. Also, just to be very clear, this position has nothing to do with the game called Twister.

The woman lies down on her side, probably her right side. The man will also be lying down on his right side, with his stomach facing the woman's stomach, but the woman will be laying head-to-toe with her man. This means that the head of the woman should be close to his feet. The couple needs to bend their left knees and raise them towards the ceiling. This will create a gap between his legs and the woman's leg.

The woman now leans forward and pushes her body through this gap so that her man's raised left leg is now above her waist, with the woman under it, but above his right leg. The woman will also be sandwiched between the man's legs with her left leg above his waist and right leg below. The man should now enter her and start thrusting.

If you think this looks complicated, you are very right, it is very complicated! It takes some practice before getting used to it.

Cross Sex Position

This position is different from the Scissors positions because the man lies at right angles to the woman. With the lower body of the man under both the woman's bent legs; the woman being laid back in the Missionary position. This angle decreases chances of skin contact but allows more unique penetration angle

Anvil Sex Position

This position is a variation of the missionary position. It's a very easy transition from the missionary position. Read careful before trying out as not to accidentally hurt.

The woman need lays on her back, like she would when in the missionary position. Just like when she is in the missionary position, the woman needs to spread her legs. But instead of her resting them on the bed, she needs to pull them close to her chest. The man then positions himself over the woman. But instead of resting on his elbows, he will be resting on his hands. With the help of her man, she positions her legs so that her calves/ankles are resting on his shoulders on either side of his neck.

Deck Chair Sex Position

In this position, the woman lays on her back, and pivots her hips so that her legs is in the air, and then she bends her knees while the man enters from a kneeling position while supporting some of his weight on the woman's legs. This position is a favorite of many men because of the sense of power that comes from folding their lover; this position doesn't leave the receiver out of the fun. When the man leans on the woman's legs, it better improves the angle of penetration to better target the g-spot, and increase satisfaction of the woman

Bent Spoon Sex Position

This position is a variant of the Acrobat position; it is also one of the favorite positions for intimacy. Unlike its much related family, regular Rear Entry, the Bent Spoon offers incredible access to the woman's chest and neck while offering less penetration angle. To be in this position, the man lies on the bed with the woman lying on top in line with her, facing the same way and with knees bent. Since the woman doesn't have very much leverage, movement is mainly the man's responsibility.

Brute Sex Position

This position is a variation of the Reverse Amazon sex position, this time with the man on top; the Brute Sex position may be one of the tougher man-on-top positions. It is not the easiest position to do, but it does give the man a sense of control and power that is absent or low in most other positions.

To perform position, the man squats over the woman (facing away) while resting on the back of the woman's legs, which is brought towards their chest to expose them at a unique angle. If the man is comfortable with his balance, he can reach behind and under to give the woman some additional manual stimulation.

Sliding Lady Sex Position

This position is like a reversal of the Coital Alignment Technique. Instead of the man being on the top of the woman, the woman I on top in this position.

Though this sex position looks a little awkward, but it can be incredibly pleasurable!

The man lies down on his back as if he was doing the Side Saddle positions or the Asian Cowgirl. The woman then needs to straddle the man as she would when doing the Cowgirl position. So she will be on her knees on top of her man, facing him. Then she needs to lean over him and rest her weight on her hands. This next one is the most crucial part:

END

Thank you for reading my book. If you enjoyed it, won't you please take a moment to look at my other titles?

Thanks!

Roman Alyssa